A Tale of Two Sides

Vienna Vercelli

ISBN 979-8-88943-619-5 (paperback)
ISBN 979-8-88943-620-1 (digital)

Christian Faith Publishing
832 Park Avenue
Meadville, PA 16335
www.christianfaithpublishing.com

Printed in the United States of America

Chapter 1

Understanding the Beginning

People say there are two sides to every story. I say there are two perspectives to every side. We all have a journey to embark on in our lives. The journey has many pathways we can take given the decisions we make. God gave us free will, but he also said, "Ask and it shall be given you; seek, and ye shall find; knock, and it shall be opened unto you" (Matthew 7:7). What I have learned is it doesn't always show up the way we think it should. We have to see the beauty in the arena we are given to find the path that leads to the door worth knocking on. The question is, how do you get there when we are seeking and yet not finding? There are many verses in scripture that speak of patience. Patience has never been a virtue of mine but is also something the Lord is. As we look back through history, biblically or not, we can agree on time. The Lord has given us time, but what do we do with it? One could argue life is short, but if we use the time we have been given for good, life is actually long. The problem is we dwell on things of our past that started in our childhood, veering our intended path a little at a time. We can play the blame game all day, but in all reality, we are no different from those in the Bible who suffered yet still stayed strong in the Lord, so why don't we? We always want the Lord to prove to us when we call upon him, but we also do not acknowledge him when he shows up nor do we bask in his glory when he presents unexpected opportunities. We chop it up to our own doings and forget they are miracles we probably didn't deserve. He gives us gifts we are all born with, we may not understand these gifts as children and as we grow, we lose focus until one day we look back and realize we have taken for granted something so special. Mine was the gift of vision.

Growing up in an extremely catholic atmosphere, I had questions. I was a super inquisitive child, not very sociable, and quite timid, well until I reached my teenage years. I was approximately the age of five, and I had one friend; unfortunately, this friend was a spirit, but I didn't know. She was real to me. We played very well together until one day she was gone. As I got a little older and attended Sunday school, I became more and more interested in learning more about Jesus. I would ask questions no one would answer; therefore, I just grabbed a Bible in my house and started reading. I read the Bible cover to cover at the age of approximately thirteen; now I didn't understand most of what I read, but Jesus knew I wanted to know more and if he was real. He revealed himself so elegantly to me in many ways. I was in the car with my mom, and we were driving down the highway. I looked up on what was a sunny day and not a cloud in the sky. I saw angels appear, and it was so mesmerizing. I will never forget the image of them rising into heaven. The goldish glow of the aura surrounding them was magnificent, I couldn't take my eyes off them. I will also never forget how he saved me more than once. While I was reading through the Bible, I remember visions of the devil chasing me, and every time I prayed my way through the dream, Jesus came. I remember one very vivid dream, in particular, where I was praying to banish the devil, and Jesus appeared behind me. He was standing on a rock over a stream, and a rainbow appeared behind him. I felt peaceful and no longer afraid, but I can still see him in my head his robes, his features, and even his shoes. Now these may have been just preconceived notions of what Jesus looks like as we have pictures everywhere of what artists have depicted he looks like. The important part here is the peace that was overwhelming in a dream state, that's how I knew Jesus was real. He never left me, so why did I choose to walk a path that didn't follow his footsteps?

Walking down the paths we choose, whether we are following God, we think we are following God, or are just lost and wondering we find ourselves talking to him. We could be talking just to talk, praying for something, regardless if it's selfish or not, angry, sad, joyful, or jokingly, but he's listening to us all time. I feel the stages of grief apply to more than just death. If we think about our day-to-day lives and the roller coaster we ride consistently, some days we love life, and we feel like nothing can stop us. On other days, we are begging and pleading, bargaining with God for whatever tragic event is happening at that moment. Sometimes we just accept because we can't see any other way and move on. Are we ever really consistent with anything we do? Abraham was consistent, he never wavered even when God tested him to sacrifice his son. "Take your son, your only son Isaac, whom you love, and go to the land of Moriah, and offer him there as a burnt offering on one of the mountains of which I shall tell you" (Genesis 22:2) Abraham did it, could you? Could you take your child knowingly to their death not knowing you would be stopped? Not many would not be able to. Those who are consistent in prayer are more apt to understand God's calling. Being steadfast in faith is different from being constant in prayer. We, who are willing to say, "Jesus is my Lord and Savior," sometimes don't always live the way we preach. Not for lack of trying, but more likely from a weakness of something easier.

Chapter 2

Where Do Decisions Come From

Decisions in every form have an outcome. However, we make decisions from the information we are given. The given information is interpreted and processed differently by each person. This is where perception becomes reality. A story is being told about a woman who has been physically abused, and it's our first instinct to think, *Why would she stay?* Then you hear the rest of the story about a young girl at the age of fifteen who falls in love for the first time, and unbeknownst to her, she is being manipulated into believing this is normal as the young mind is still open and vulnerable, now it's hard to get away. We can tell the same story in a completely different way that enables our minds to wonder. Once we process this information, we identify things about the story to our own life experiences. This is where empathy comes in. I was relatively quiet until the age of fifteen, so where did the big change come in? When I met the boy, I fell in love with. What we don't realize when we are that young how vulnerable we really are. It shapes us into young adults, but how do you properly explain to a teenager their choices today build bridges for the path they are heading? "Children obey, your parents in the Lord: for this is right" (Ephesians 6:1). It is written, and yet we still cannot reason with a teenager. Their reality is built on their stimulating surroundings just like kids and adults. Although, as parents, I think we forget about the world they live in and expect them to just listen without listening to them. We don't always have to agree with the logic or reasoning behind what they say, but maybe if we made our children feel comfortable enough to trust us, they would admit their struggles and look for help. For example, a teenage girl who feels lost and rejected, like she can't do anything right, will rebel in different ways just as the Israelites rebelled with a golden calf for not getting the proper attention they desired. Do we really get to decide bad attention is better than no attention? You can see it two different ways: just as the Israelites felt they were abandoned and turned to a new idol, teenagers have no self-control, but God never ignored them just as our parents were not ignoring us. So why do we feel the need to rebel? Is it the paths we cross as we go down unknown roads and encounter unforeseen circumstances where we make hasty decisions we tend to regret later? What are considered turning points when we make decisions based on the situation we are put in? Is it when you have an uncle who comes to live with you and is unknowingly doing drugs in the house who is discovered by the teenager who, at the time, couldn't see past her own selfishness? Therefore no one is told because he never really bothered her before the day, he asked her to watch an unfathomable event, that changed her course. Hindsight is twenty-twenty!

How is a child supposed to understand what a parent is dealing with and how is a parent supposed to deal with circumstances and still give their very best to the child? This seems to be the real disconnect in a parental relationship. Yet Jesus walked the earth and experienced what we experience, never wavered once from his Father, our Father, and we can't even have a decent relationship with our earthly parents? The cycle appears to be never-ending until the day Jesus returns. Psychologists and psychiatrists always start back at the beginning. How far back can you remember your first traumatic event? What is traumatic to you? Is it when you see your mom being thrown around a kitchen by her sister and slammed into the walls, and no one does anything to help her? Or is it when your cousin pins you into a room at a family event on multiple occasions and exposes himself while trying to make you touch him inappropriately?

We search for reasoning and logic behind the stories we hear and the circumstances we see. What if there is no logic behind things that are real? What if we make immediate decisions in a moment due to the position, we feel we are in? Although the reality may be very different from the experience, but if the situation feels real and we are looking for a way out, are we not taught to survive? What if you find yourself at seventeen looking for anyone to love you and keep you safe because your father took off and your mother is now living with a perverted man? We can only see one side when we are in a situation ourselves. Once we are able to see the whole picture, we can see the mother and father encountering their own realities and surviving their own stories. It's a vicious cycle that enables the hamster wheel we cannot seem to get out of. How? What if your story is about a young girl who gets married and has a baby at eighteen, only to be beaten so badly, you almost lose the baby and you can't go home because your father won't let you, and now you are pregnant and alone? You do what you have to in order to survive and provide for your child. Some years later, you meet a man who appears to be normal, in such a way that is not physically abusive. He's charming, adores your child, and is nonthreatening. You eventually trust him, fall in love, and get married. He willingly adopts your child, and then you have another with him. He's not perfect, but he's safe, so you deal with his faults knowing you have your own and convince yourself it's not really that bad. Some years later, things even out, and you are really just happy for many years. You feel like, *Finally God has answered my prayers*, and it's smooth sailing from here. "The Lord gives strength to his people, and the Lord blesses his people with peace" (Psalm 29:11). Unknowingly it was the calm before another storm. Being the family person you are and longing for the family life you always wanted as a kid, you allow your child to move back in with her boyfriend because they are struggling financially, and then your great aunt who now can longer live by herself, and then finally your husband's brother who needs a place to live for a while because he was hurt and is out of work. Now you have four new people in your house to take care of not including your sixteen-year-old daughter, but God calls us to help those in need, right? "Those who are gracious to the poor lend to the Lord, and the Lord will fully repay them" (Proverbs 19:17). Although you are now so entrenched in the hectic life of taking care of others that your sixteen-year-old gets lost in the woods. From the outside looking in, you could insinuate she is a teenager, and she will grow out it, but from the inside looking out, all you want to do is scream. Are families what you consider cursed from the beginning? The very first murder in the Bible is at the hands of his own brother. Friends and family seem to be the worst enemies, do we not treat them wretchedly? However, we treat strangers and neighbors with love and respect. "Everyone who hates his brother is a murderer, and you know that no murderer has eternal life abiding in him" (1 John 3:15). Do we treat family and friends as enemies because of jealousy as Cane did by killing Abel, Joseph's brothers did by selling him, and Judas did by betraying Jesus for thirty pieces of silver? "But if anyone does not provide for his relatives, and especially for members of his household, he has denied the faith and is worse than an unbeliever" (1 Timothy 5:8). Are we unbelievers trying to make things right in our own minds by helping strangers and treating them better than we treat our own family and friends? "Thou shalt love the Lord thy God with all thy heart, and with all thy soul, and with all thy mind. This is the first and great commandment. And the second is like unto it, Thou shalt love thy neighbor as thyself" (Matthew 22:37–39). As the commandment says we are to love our neighbor as ourselves most of us love ourselves, sometimes a little too much where arrogance comes into play, but still, is this why we treat strangers better than family? Scripture depicts many scenarios of families hurting each other in different ways. "A friend loves at all times, and a brother is born for a time of adversity" (Proverbs 17:17). Depending on how you interpret the verse, you can see a pattern of scripture and how we operate as humans.

Chapter 3

Deciphering Moments

Sometimes we discover as we go through things and become more aware that the adversity we are encountering is God bringing us back to a more humble position. We tend to rely more on God's help when we feel the disparity, and when he blesses us at first, we are grateful but then eventually take him for granted. Maybe this is his way of saying, "Don't forget who you are and where you came from."

Scripture discusses seasons and hardships in many scenarios. We journey through scripture in each season we are experiencing is when we find solitude for the situation at hand. It appears we can view the same story in the Bible in different ways depending on the problem we are currently facing. "There is a time for everything, and a season for every activity under the heavens" (Ecclesiastes 3:1). Being in the midst of a marriage where your partner has been unfaithful and emotions are strong scripture tells us a wife is not to leave her husband or she can never remarry. But for those who are married, I have a command that comes not from me, but from the Lord. "A wife must not leave her husband. But if she does leave him, let her remain single or else be reconciled to him" (1 Corinthians 7:10–17), which we can conclude that regardless of what happened, infidelity or not, the woman is not allowed to leave a man, or she will either be single forever or return to her husband. However, if a man marries a woman who becomes displeasing to him because he finds something indecent about her, and he writes her a certificate of divorce, gives it to her, and sends her from his house, and if after she leaves his house, she becomes the wife of another man, and her second husband dislikes her and writes her a certificate of divorce, gives it to her, and sends her from his house, or if he dies, then her first husband, who divorced her, is not allowed to marry her again after she has been defiled. That would be detestable in the eyes of the Lord. Do not bring sin upon the land the Lord your God is giving you as an inheritance (Deuteronomy 24:1–4). Do we see the irony? Are we supposed to assume based on feelings at the moment which verse to relate our situation to? How do we know if, as a woman, we are allowed to remarry or not remarry? Do we know what is pleasing to the Lord? God created man and woman alike; he created a woman to free man from loneliness. The Lord God said, "It is not good for the man to be alone. I will make a helper suitable for him." Now the Lord God had formed out of the ground all the wild animals and all the birds in the sky. He brought them to the man to see what he would name them, and whatever the man called each living creature, that was its name. So the man gave names to all the livestock, the birds in the sky, and all the wild animals. But for Adam, no suitable helper was found. So the Lord God caused the man to fall into a deep sleep, and while he was sleeping, he took one of the man's ribs and then closed up the place with flesh. Then the Lord God made a woman from the rib he had taken out of the man, and he brought her to the man (Genesis 2:18–22). God didn't want a man to be alone, and it can be portrayed that he gave man many options on how to treat a woman. From good to bad. However, we can also presume not so many choices for the woman.

The Lord made Adam first and saw he was lonely. He made Eve from Adams's flesh and bone. We hear about prostitution in the Bible, and of course, it is relevant today, but what we don't read about is how those girls got there and how they are probably doing it against their will. What we don't hear is the girl was probably molested at a young age or kidnapped and sold into it with no way out. What we don't hear is she has probably had a long line of men in her life who have touched her inappropriately, and she felt she had nowhere to turn, so if the men who are supposed to keep her safe treat her this way, then what's the point of fighting off the rest of the men in the world. Isn't that like the old expression "If you can't beat them, join them"? It's still not pleasurable; it's still considered against her will. It's just not presented that way. Isn't perspective all about how we tell the story? Isn't that why good lawyers can provide reasonable doubt in a case? "Husbands, love your wives, as Christ loved the church and gave himself up for her, that he might sanctify her, having cleansed her by the washing of water with the word, so that he might present the church to himself in splendor, without spot or wrinkle or any such thing, that she might be holy and without blemish. In the same way husbands should love their wives as their own bodies. He who loves his wife loves himself. For no one ever hated his own flesh, but nourishes and cherishes it, just as Christ does the church" (Ephesians 5:25–29). Why do men torture women when it's written they are supposed to cherish and love them as if we were their own bodies? No one is asking what are the events that led to her prostitution. Was it when her father came at her? Or her sister's fiancé that would constantly insist on deplorable gestures. No one is questioning in the Bible Mary Magdalene, but she is portrayed as a prostitute, yet Jesus made her a disciple. Not only did he make her a disciple, he appeared to her first when he rose from his crucifixion. How do we go from one verse telling us if a woman is displeasing to the man, he is allowed to leave her and give her to another man, to another verse telling us that the same man is supposed to protect and cherish that woman as if she is his own flesh and blood. Is this why we have so much confusion in the world on how a relationship should be? We can interpret these verses in many ways to fit our perceived theory on the matter, but what we should be really asking is how do we know what is really pleasing of the Lord and his vision for us?

Chapter 4

Relativity of Perspective

Every time we revisit a verse in scripture, we relate it to the given circumstance and create a story that is appealing to the mind and call it a life lesson. Is this because we can construe scripture to paint a picture suitable for the weary?

While we chop things up to life lessons, the Lord does speak of wisdom. We have the tools literally given to us, and yet we do not utilize them to teach our children properly at a young age. If any of you lacks wisdom, he should ask God, who gives generously to all without finding fault, and it will be given to him (James 1:5). We all lack wisdom at a young age, but if we learn to ask and seek, then maybe our lives would take different courses. What course would your life take if we chose how to depict scripture differently starting at a young age?

Suppose your child says, "Mom, is Starbucks a sin? I heard that the siren is the logo, and we shouldn't drink it anymore." Or "Mom, is rap a sin? I heard it sinful to listen to rap." Well, if you really think about it, yes, it is all a sin, but if you counted how many times in a day you sin, basically everything we do is sinful. Then she continues with, "I heard that when you get to heaven that Jesus says if you don't know his name, then you really never knew me and he turns you away." The problem with interpretation is that the same story means different things to different people. So you say, "Well, scripture says there is only one unforgivable sin, and it is blasphemy against the Holy Spirit."

"And I tell you, every sin and blasphemy will be forgiven men, but the blasphemy against the spirit will not be forgiven. Anyone who speaks a word against the Son of man will be forgiven, but anyone who speaks against the Holy Spirit will not be forgiven, either in this age or in the age to come" (Matthew 12:31–32). Do you try to avoid sin? Of course. Do you try to make good choices based on God's word? Yes. John, Acts, Matthew, Peter, Romans, etc.—all have versus that suggest repentance, forgiveness, and mercy from the Lord.

"If we confess our sins, he is faithful and just to forgive us our sins and to cleanse us from all unrighteousness" (1 John 1:9). Now it's not to say go and sin then repent but use the free will God has given us for good, and if we make a mistake, repent because he gave his only Son so that we may have eternal life with him. Trying to put things in perspective for a teenager asking questions about Jesus and wondering if the world around her is just as confused as she is. Although she wants desperately to know exactly what Jesus wants and it's not always easy when you don't know yourself. However, you are also trying desperately to do what pleases God and not really sure if you are doing it right, because at eighteen years old, your found yourself working in nightclubs to pay bills after your parents divorced, your dad left, and you made assumptions that your mother was cheating based on the perceived situation happening in front of your eyes. You later find out about your mother's reality and move in with her and her new boyfriend. The boyfriend, who turns out later to be a real creep, with his inappropriate comments and suggestive advice to work as an exotic dancer while he brings your mother to watch you dance. Although you feel uncomfortable, you know you are not participating in undesirable behavior while working. You meet a boy who later proposes, and you end up pregnant. You are scared but reveal the situation to your mom and her boyfriend who proceed to call you a whore and tell you to get out. Now the feeling of hopelessness consumes you, and you have an abortion that you never recover from. When you are taught from a young age that it's a sin, how do you forgive yourself? Although the Bible doesn't specifically mention abortion, it does define a life for a life. "If men strive, and hurt a woman with child, so that her fruit depart from her, and yet no mischief follow: he shall be surely punished, according as the woman's husband will lay upon him; and he shall pay as the judges determine. And if any mischief follow, then thou shalt give life for life, eye for eye, tooth for tooth, hand for hand, foot for foot, burning for burning, wound for wound, stripe for stripe" (Exodus 21:22–25). Well, who is to say the one having the abortion is or isn't technically taking the life, does that person deserve to live? Although, according to scripture Blasphemy against the Holy Spirit is the only unforgivable sin. "Then I acknowledged my sin to You and did not hide my iniquity. I said, 'I will confess my transgressions to the LORD' and You forgave the guilt of my sin" (Psalm 32:5).

What is blasphemy against the Holy Spirit? Is it taking the Lord's name in vain? Is it denying the Lord publicly or even privately? Is it preaching the Lord's Word and not abiding by his laws? "Not everyone who says to me, "Lord, Lord' will enter the kingdom of Heaven, but the one who does the will of my Father who is in heaven. On that day many will say to me Lord, Lord did we not prophesy in your name, and cast out demons in your name, and do may mighty works in your name? And the will I declare to them, I never knew you; depart from me, you workers of lawlessness" (Matthew 7:21–23).

If your perspective is your reality, then how does it become a lie just because someone else doesn't see it the same way? A lie is something of deceit with a premeditated answer. "Everyone utters lies to his neighbor; with flattering lips and a double heart they speak" (Psalm 12:2). How do we tell what is a perceived reality and what is a lie? We don't. My grandmother used to say, "Lies have legs." I like to think that metaphor is true as God will reveal things and show us signs if we pay attention to him. Although, going back to patience, sometimes he makes us wait to see the truth maybe because the person has to experience something similar in order to see the truth and appreciate it rather than hear it and dismiss it as a lie. Deciphering your reality based on your circumstances and yet from the outside looking in, you have others telling you a different story. Is this where depression starts?

Chapter 5

Depression

Depression is something most of us have suffered from or are currently suffering from. The present is something we are supposed to live in every day. We are supposed to repent of past mistakes remember God is with us always and not worry about the future because he will take care of it for us. So don't worry about tomorrow, for tomorrow will bring its own worries. Today's trouble is enough for today (Matthew 6:34). Yet it's our past and future that consume us. In the future, we worry about how we are going to pay our bills or feed our families. The Israelites survived in the desert for forty years living on manna that came daily and dissipated overnight for those that tried to hoard it except for the Sabbath day, proving God is always providing. According to the Gospel of John, Jesus also fed five thousand followers with two fish and five loaves of bread. We have so many accounts of God being here in our present situation, providing and guiding, and yet we still ignore it. "How long will they refuse to believe in me, in spite of all the miraculous signs I have performed among them? I will strike them down with a plague and destroy them" (Numbers 14:11). Why is God always having to prove himself to us; he doesn't have to and yet still continues to. We choose to look for worldly answers more than his. Is this why we have ailments? Is this the plague we suffer from?

Depression stems from many things the past, present, and future. The past that we dwell on from events that have happened to us and cannot change or forget. Therefore, we end up with regrets, or if the event was traumatic, PTSD. Scripture says, "Forget the former things; do not dwell on the past. See I am doing a new thing! Now it springs up; do you not perceive it? I am making a way in the wilderness and streams in the wasteland" (Isaiah 43:18–19). So how do we forget things that are embedded in our minds? Time? Time is said to heal all things, right? Possibly, but what really is time? It's a moment, and it's endless in the same scenario.

Memories were given to us as a gift to remind us to praise him every day. "Making the most of every opportunity, because the days are evil" (Ephesians 5:16). The days of evil will come to an end eventually, and Jesus wants us to remember our sins so we repent, but with that comes the ability to remember the awful things that have happened to us as well. "Remember therefore from where you have fallen; repent and do the first works, or else I will come to you quickly and remove your lampstand from its place—unless you repent" (Revelation 2:5). Is there a trick to forgetting some things and remembering others? Some could argue that's why we have addicts, whether its drugs or alcohol, or that's why there are depression medications. Realistically we all have coping mechanisms. Mine is alcohol. Noah was depicted to be a drunk. "He drank of the wine and became drunk and lay uncovered in his tent" (Genesis 9:21), but why? Was he depressed, even though God chose him to build the Ark?

Depression is seen throughout the Bible as Believers we know these stories, and yet we still turn away from the Word of God and turn to resources, not of his will. We see Elijah afraid and filled with hopelessness, David filled with fear and guilt, Jonah's anger driving him to flee, and Moses desperately wanting to quit. We all have felt these emotions at some point in our lives if we are not living it now. Depression has consumed me over the years, but where does it stem from, and when does it end? I have felt as Jeremiah felt, cursed, but also have felt blessed. However, it feels as if it is a constant inner battle, and I never know which side is going win on which day. Will

I wake up feeling blessed and strong in the Lord or will I wake up feeling weak and spiritually drained? "The Lord is close to the brokenhearted and saves those who are crushed in spirit" (Psalm 34:18). Emotional despair and fear is what bring us close to the Lord, but scripture tells us to rejoice! (Philippians 4:4). "Rejoice in the Lord always; again I will say, Rejoice" (1 Thessalonians 5:16). "Rejoice always" (Romans 15:13). "May the God of hope fill you with all joy and peace in believing, so that by the power of the holy spirit you may abound in hope." No wonder depression is deep-rooted in our souls. It feels like a constant roller coaster of emotions, but no one has suffered more than Jesus, so why do we complain? Do we really have reason to validate our feelings? Our creator gave us a garden with everything we could ever need, we ruined it. God forgave us, giving us more chances and finally giving us everlasting life, and all we have to do is accept him and love him. Our worldly desires are what ultimately keep us on this rollercoaster. God knew of this path before we created it as Lucifer made his jealousy known and his intentions clear that he was not going down without a fight, and we wonder why we are always on the brink of another war. We as humans will always fight for power until the day Jesus returns and reveals the real kingdom of heaven.

Chapter 6

Circumstantial Struggles

When we are young, we pretty much hear the same Bible verses over and over. We hear the story of David defeating Goliath. We hear the story of Noah and how he built the Ark and saved his family and all the land animals. We hear the story of Moses and how he took on the king to free the people of Jerusalem as God requested and how Jonah was saved by being swallowed and expelled on land. What if we are doing it all wrong? What if we told the whole story and brought to light the challenges they faced and how God saved them from their inner struggles? The emotional responses to mental battles we all face at some point in our lives. Would we be able to deal with depression differently? Could we prevent some of the suicides, murders, and addiction problems we see so much of? Would we see depression differently and the coping mechanisms, such as drugs and alcohol that play a big part in dealing with depression, but what if we learned at a young age that when we encounter things in the future, we know that there is hope, instead of turning to drugs or alcohol first, killing ourselves or murdering someone because we see no other way at the moment? What if we had the knowledge and ability to remind ourselves that Noah had a drinking problem and God saved him or Jonah was angry and God still gave him a second chance? Would we be more apt to seek God's help first? Would we be more in tune to ask God for a second chance instead of turning to alternative methods to relieve the emotional pain we are experiencing?

Although it's not a solution to every situation we are faced with in our lives. They say God doesn't call the righteous, but he calls the broken. How broken do we have to be to see him? Is it when you are raped and do not tell anyone because he was also the man you gave your virginity to? Is it when you are molested by the man who is supposed to protect you and keep you safe? Is it when you cry yourself to sleep at night praying for God to just take you because you cannot see another way? Joseph was sold into slavery and Job lost everything he had, but God eventually blessed them ten times over. However, they suffered before they were blessed. We wonder why God is always testing us and our faith in him, but we are always seeking proof of his existence too. It's very contradictory. Have you ever tried to bargain with God to prove something to you, and in exchange, you'll pray more or stop doing something you know you shouldn't be doing anyway? I think we can all relate to this. We are all searching for purpose or meaning or reasoning by the situations we encounter in life. "As I have planned, so shall it be, and as I have purposed, so shall it stand" (Isaiah 14:24). We are searching for what our purpose is, and this leads us down paths that shape us in different ways. While we feel inspired some days when an idea or person presents itself, we think, everything happens for a reason, right? But what are we really focused on? Ourselves, our goals, and what we think we need. God tries to push us down his path, but if we can't see his feet, how are we really to follow? How do we overcome the impurities that happen to us as kids and not take that into our adult reality? Our perception is altered at an age of innocence and carried through our years. Depression, thoughts of suicide, and feelings of hopelessness consume us to which we live in fear but not fear of the Lord as it should be, fear of life itself. God created this amazing world and did not have to bring us into it. He created man last. God chose to give us this glorious life, and yet we take it for granted every day just as our ancestors named in the Bible. Noah was 950 years old according to scripture, and God chose him to save a few. Then we repeated history, and God said no more. "My spirit shall not abide in man forever, for he is flesh; his days shall be a hundred and twenty years" (Genesis 6:3). It is our sins that have numbered our days for God's love is pure, but his patience with man is limited. Although we continue to destroy ourselves and the earth that was so graciously given to us to rule, God has never broken his promises to us. Abraham was promised multiple descendants and land for years to come. Moses was promised freedom to the Israelites, and God guided them safely. God fulfilled his promise to Solomon by granting him honor as he was known as Israel's greatest king and wisdom as it was said people came from afar to interpret his knowledge and one of my favorites is God's promise to never flood the earth again, even giving us the constant reminder with a rainbow every time it rains. "I have set my rainbow in the clouds, and it will be the sign of the covenant between me and the earth. Whenever I bring clouds over the earth and the rainbow appears in the clouds, I will remember my covenant between me and you and all living creatures of every kind. Never again will the waters become a flood to destroy all life" (Genesis 9:13–15). Nevertheless, we cannot seem to keep ourselves out of trouble. We continue to view our circumstances looking back instead of starting from the beginning, teaching our children the importance of choices, and allowing God to guide the journey in order to fulfill the quest.

Chapter 7

Lens of Compassion

"Bear with each other and forgive one another if any of you has a griev-ance against someone. Forgive as the Lord forgave you" (Colossians 3:13). In order to forgive, do we not look for a logical reason to forgive that person? Why? God didn't put boundaries on our for-giveness. He didn't say, give me a reason to forgive you. "The Lord our God is merciful and forgiving, even though we have rebelled against him" (Daniel 9:9), and he sent his only son in the flesh to be crucified for us. Why do we have such a hard time forgiving each other? Maybe the better question is how do we fully forgive the way we are supposed to when the memory of the pain is still there? "For I will forgive their wickedness and will remember their sins no more" (Hebrews 8:12). If we truly forgive the sins against us, would we not lose the memory as well as the scripture has said?

The Bible has so many versions and so many interpretations of events and stories, the only thing we can know for sure is when we get to heaven, we will know the real story. Unless Jesus decides to return in our lifetime, but we can only interpret the book of Revelations as we can only interpret the rest of the scripture. What we know is Jesus will return, and there will be a final battle; Jesus will win, and we will finally have peace on earth and live in his reign forever. That is what I pray for. I pray for the return of Jesus. I pray to live in his reign. I pray the earth looks as the garden looked for Adam and Eve, and I pray for every soul to repent, believe, and accept our Lord before he comes, and there is no more time.

While interpretation may vary from person to person, we as believers have to learn to stop looking from the outside in and start empathizing with those by placing ourselves in the same orbit. We are constantly subconsciously judging those because we only see our side of the lens. "Do not judge, or you too will be judged. For in the same way you judge others, you will be judged, and with the measure you use, it will be measured to you" (Matthew 7:1–2). Judging others because they do not see through the same lens you do doesn't help anyone see Jesus. If anything, it takes our eyes off the Lord and distracts us from what the Lord has intended for us.

Distractions of this world have become the "norm," consuming ourselves in these distractions is what take us from immersing ourselves in the Word of God. TikTok, Instagram, Facebook, Twitter, etc. We are more focused on what everyone else is doing in the world rather than on how we can serve the Lord, but that's just my perspective. Engrossed with worldly activities six days a week only to go to church on Sunday to make your soul feel better for Monday. God made the world in six days and rested on the seventh. God said "For the world offers only a craving for physical pleasure, a craving for everything we see, and pride in our achievements and possessions. These are not from the Father but are from this world" (1 John 2:16).

How do we really know the path we are on is the one God chose for us? We justify things that we see as signs of being on the right path, but perspective has a way that can manipulate a situation into anything you want it to be. Isn't the old saying "the greatest trick the Devil ever played was to convince the world he didn't exists"? Justification can be applied to any circumstance. The real path is what matters though. How do you get on the right path when the lens you are looking through has been so corrupted? "Search me, God, and know my heart; test me and know my anxious thoughts. See if there is any offensive way in me, and lead me in the way everlasting" (Psalm 139:23–24). Everlasting life in the Lord is what we yearn for believers and unbelievers alike. Unbelievers are searching for something they just want, something scientific they can prove.

Well, theory has proven many things including the existence of Jesus. However, unbelievers will justify that with science too.

Do we use the circumstances we participate in to tell a story that is inspiring others to find Jesus? When we help others, are we trying to help ourselves feel better? Are we trying to right the wrongs we have done? Or do we do it to please God? How do we really know the why behind what we do in this case? Some individuals can be been seen as doing it for publicity when they are constantly "showing off" their contributions. Some individuals do it behind the scene and never get recognized but are seen by God. Although, the frustration can be overwhelming when the person behind the scenes feels underappreciated but also conflicted because they didn't want the spotlight. Truly I tell you, they have received their reward in full. But when you give to the needy, do not let your left hand know what your right hand is doing so that your giving may be in secret. "Then your Father, who sees what is done in secret, will reward you" (Matthew 6:1–4). Why are there conflicting feelings when we think we are doing it for the right reasons? Living in a world full of symbolism and not wanting to be of this world but also feeling sad when no one knows what you have done.

What if we pray for signs or God to open doors, and we find ourselves struggling through the next door and the one after that, until one day we open a door we think is finally a saving grace and find out it, too, has a secret passage that led to another tunnel of disappointment? We find ourselves crying and pleading once more for God's help because the inner battle is killing you. Then you feel as if we need to revisit the doors and find out where we went wrong but also feel maybe we didn't go wrong maybe this is the door he told us to go in because he knew something you didn't and even though you feel lost and afraid, you still have a feeling that everything will be okay.

"Love is patient and kind; love does not envy or boast; it is not arrogant or rude. It does not insist on its own way; it is not irritable or resentful; it does not rejoice at wrongdoing, but rejoices with the truth. Love bears all things, believes all things, hopes all things, endures all things" (1 Corinthians 13:4–7). Love is perpetual and we use it out of context in more ways than one. We say things like "I do this out of Love" or "if you love me…" Love wasn't meant to be a crutch for people to manipulate others; it was meant for us to have empathy and passion. God wants us to be as passionate about him as he is for us. The Lord wants us to see each other the way he sees us.

Looking through the looking glass where everything is different on the other side, the lens seems so clear it gives of the version of the story meaning until we see the glass is reversed and the lens is a little cloudy. Then we realize we only saw our emotional response to an act of an unbecoming circumstance. When we alter what we focus on we can adjust the lens. However, we can't adjust the lens until we empathize with the condition. When do we realize the reality of the situation we put ourselves in?

Chapter 8

Perceptual Ignorance

There's a song that says, "There are two sides to every story, ones a lie and one the truth if you stop telling lies about me I won't tell the truth about you." When relationships fail, sometimes the anger and hurt is overwhelming and the need to vent is said to be helpful. Psychologists will tell you it's good to talk about things, it's part of the healing process. The problem lies when two people see things very differently. A spouse of sorts, whether married or dating, has their version. It doesn't mean it's a lie; it just means their perspective on what happened is how they felt when it happened. For example, a wife who has a small child and keeps finding her husband in strip clubs who can't understand why. In the moment, she feels angry and unloved because her husband has a lustful inconspicuous nature and it's killing her inside, but no matter how many times you talk to him about it, he doesn't see the issue. The Lord says, "If your brother sins against you, go and tell him his fault, between you and him alone. If he listens to you, you have gained your brother" (Matthew 18:15). Therefore, she starts to vent, but her husband doesn't feel its cheating, nor does he see the problem. Two sides to the story. Things cool down for a bit, and he finally stops going to strip clubs. Her perspective is now finally things are getting better, and then they have another child. Unknowingly during her pregnancy, he was having an affair with another woman. Now no one is questioning the perspective of the affair. However, the lack of remorse that came with the lie that was told when he was caught could be questionable. What was the reasoning behind the lie? Why did she stay? Praying about it and thinking about it, as hurt as she was, she couldn't imagine her life without him, but she needed to understand and wanted desperately to fix whatever was wrong, so she suggested therapy. He agrees, and after months of therapy, he finally admits his wrongs, but yet the remorse is still not there. Now there is no trust. How can you remain married to someone who cannot be trusted to stay faithful, but the Lord says, "Put not your trust in princes, nor in the son of man, in whom there is no help" (Psalm 146:3). We are not supposed to trust in from the outside looking in can we see two sides. What if the man is hurting but doesn't seem to know what to do or how to deal with whatever he is experiencing and it's his way of exchanging his pain for pleasure? What if he feels he doesn't want to hurt his wife so he keeps his secrets and finds alternatives to burying his pain? However, she sees it in a completely different manner. What if his childhood was one of sorrow and despair? What if he knows no other way? We can only see what is felt in a moment. Our first instinct is always, why me, or why is this person treating me this way, but we never take the time to step outside of the box and ask ourselves what is that person experiencing to make them want to act in an inappropriate manner. We can see past our own selfishness and how we are being treated in a circumstance, which leads to the perception of the experience at hand. Foolish minds create an illusion of fear.

Chapter 9

Fearfully Foolish

We do things out of fear. Fear of doing what's right and not knowing how. Fear of not knowing what's right. Fear of displeasing someone and fear of perception. Do we ever really do things in fear of God? As it should be? Sometimes we stand up for what we believe in, and sometimes we stand back and watch while others are persecuted. Fear is a finicky feeling because we don't know exactly how we are going to translate the action until it is too late. But when you ask, you must believe and not doubt, because the one who doubts is like a wave of the sea, blown and tossed by the wind. That person should not expect to receive anything from the Lord. Such a person is double-minded and unstable in all they do (James 1:6–8). Our sympathetic nervous system has what we call the fight or flight system. When fear strikes us, suddenly we take action one way or another, but our actions are not consistently fearful of the Lord. We fear the instant consequence more than the eternal one because it's not staring us in the face. Therefore, we react then repent and think our soul is good with God. Peter denied Jesus three times out fear in the moment. Even though he was Jesus's disciple and knew Jesus probably better than most of us, his fear was stronger than his faith. Is this the same exact scenario we recreate daily? Is it also not blasphemy, which is said to be the only unforgivable sin, the denial of Jesus? Yet we know Peter repented and was forgiven. "The Lord turned and looked straight at

Peter. Then Peter remembered the word the Lord had spoken to him: Before the rooster crows today, you will disown me three times. And he went outside and wept bitterly" (Luke 22:61–62). It is written Jesus appeared to the disciples including Peter; the third time was at the Sea of Tiberias where Peter went fishing, and the Lord provided an abundance of fish and then told them to eat.

When they had finished eating, Jesus said to Simon Peter, "Simon son of John, do you love me more than these?"

"Yes, Lord," he said, "you know that I love you."

Jesus said, "Feed my lambs." Again Jesus said, "Simon son of John, do you love me?"

He answered, "Yes, Lord, you know that I love you."

Jesus said, "Take care of my sheep." The third time, he said to him, "Simon, son of John, do you love me?" Peter was hurt because Jesus asked him the third time, "Do you love me?"

He said, "Lord, you know all things; you know that I love you." Jesus said, "Feed my sheep. (John 21:15–17).

This screams hope and forgiveness. This tells a story that Jesus wants us all to be with him even though we constantly sin against his wishes. He shows us throughout history, all we have to do is ask for forgiveness. Real forgiveness, an utterly remorseful cry for his love and mercy. When we hit that moment and the peace finally consumes us to where we know he is with us, we fail him again in a vicious cycle of the worldly battle of domination. We know Jesus is coming back, and he's coming back with vengeance to save his people once again. Yet we can't seem to fight for him the way he fights for us, "that at the name of Jesus every knee should bow, in heaven and on earth and under the earth, and every tongue acknowledge that Jesus Christ is Lord, to the glory of God the Father" (Philippians 2:10–11). Now we can argue that we do fight and there are those who are putting their lives in the middle of this biblical war we have going on currently with the different religions. *Religion* is such a broad word anymore. It speaks to too many godly creatures. Why do we call ourselves Christian when Jesus was Hebrew? I just call myself a believer in Christ. I believe in the Lord Jesus as my Lord and Savior; that's all I know to be true. Anything outside of this is just theory with so many versions of the Bible floating around and so many scrolls and books that were pulled by different organizations. We will all one day be blessed with his presence, but will we live with him in eternity? "For if God did not spare angels when they sinned, but sent them to hell, putting them in chains of darkness to be held for judgment" (Peter 2:4).

Chapter 10

Creating Chaos

While each version of our journey has new roads and we wander through the trails making judgment calls, reflecting years later to only discover our choices are what really created the chaos, no matter who we want to blame or how we want to portray the story, all relevant situations are caused by the choices we make. We just need to learn to stop reacting immediately and think, pray, and be patient. While we think about the circumstances that potentially have unavoidable repercussions, such as a robbery. Is it our fault if we walked into the bank or store and moments later, a robbery happens? No, of course not. It's the choices we make during and after the situation that pre-determines the next path we go down. However, it's the fear and the emotional response that takes over in the moment that we can or cannot control. Some could argue we can control our responses and some would argue we can't. We can take into consideration those who have practiced self-control to a point where maybe they have learned how to handle circumstances that someone else may call difficult. Perspective is two people in the same scenario creating two different realities. A married couple living in the same house, has a couple of kids, good jobs, and what we would call a nice life; one person is happy, life is great; the other person is sad, and no one knows why. What is wrong? What is causing the sorrow? Why does is seem as if there is no meaning to life? Searching for purpose and meaning to things we can't control can consume our minds and bring prenotions of what's expected next. However, we have to remember the bad things are nothing more than the Devil fighting for our souls. We can't see it in the moment. We say things like "Why me, Lord?" We look for answers that we think God is putting us through, but he is really not putting us through anything. We are our definition of chaos. A new perspective that could be painfully true is the "what if" scenario. What if we stop blaming others for the path we chose? What if we looked at the choices we made and took responsibility? Would we still make the same choices if we didn't have someone else to blame?

A Rubix cube can arguably be one of the toughest puzzles to solve. We make adjustments based on how we see the picture flipping it around continuously until we either complete it with all sides being perfectly matched or get frustrated and toss it to the side for another day. As we navigate through life looking at the different scenarios presented to us, we make decisions and adjust or adapt, there is an exploratory period every time we change the scene. Ultimately we continue to change the pattern based on our emotions at the moment trying to solve the ultimate puzzle. Peace! All we are really searching for in life is peace. Inner peace is something we all desire but cannot say we have. "Lord, you establish peace for us; all that we have accomplished, you have done for us" (Isaiah 26:12). We have days where we can say we are at peace but to truly be at peace every day with no inner demons or thoughts is rare and remarkable all in one. Each of us has a maze to wander through or a puzzle to solve depending on your perspective. Remember the journey is always about Jesus, and whether you are one of the lost, the found, or still seeking, Yahweh will always open doors to another chapter.

Forever in your thoughts,

Vienna Vercelli

About the Author

Vienna Vercelli, like every child had a dream and aspirations. Sometimes those dreams become reality as people grow and sometimes obstacles hinder the path. From the outside looking in we can see a young girl who appears to have just made bad decisions, but from the other side of the glass, you can see a girl who feels scared. The expression "Never judge a book by its cover" has a deeper meaning when you see the perception from a new angle. While we know judgment is only of the Lord, do we not judge each other constantly with our own opinions? Depression doesn't start in the beginning it develops through time.